CRYPTOCURRENCY

Cryptocurrency Basics, Bitcoin, Blockchain and Trading Cryptocurrency – How to Buy, Invest, Sell, and Store Cryptocurrency

© Copyright - Lee Sebastian
All Rights Reserved

Published By:
Positive Impact Books

Join Our Book Community To Get
FREE Book Promotion, Alerts and Discounts
When Announced.

https://PositiveImpactBooks.com

Legal Disclaimer

The following Book is produced below with the goal of providing information that is as accurate and reliable as possible. Regardless, purchasing this Book can be seen as consent to the fact that both the publisher and the author of this book are in no way experts on the topics discussed within and that any recommendations or suggestions that are made herein are for entertainment purposes only. Professionals should be consulted as needed prior to undertaking any of the action endorsed herein.

This declaration is deemed fair and valid by both the American Bar Association and the Committee of Publishers Association and is legally binding throughout the United States.

Furthermore, the transmission, duplication or reproduction of any of the following work including specific information will be considered an illegal act irrespective of if it is done electronically or in print. This extends to creating a secondary or tertiary copy of the work or a recorded copy and is only allowed with the express written consent of the Publisher. All additional rights reserved.

The information in the following pages is broadly considered to be a truthful and accurate account of facts and as such any inattention, use or misuse of the information in question by the reader will render any resulting actions solely under their purview. There are no scenarios in which the publisher or the original author of this work can be in any fashion deemed liable for any hardship or damages that may befall them after undertaking information described herein.

Additionally, the information in the following pages is intended only for informational purposes and should thus be thought of as universal. As befitting its nature, it is presented without assurance regarding its prolonged validity or interim quality. Trademarks that are mentioned are done without written consent and can in no way be considered an endorsement from the trademark holder.

Table of Contents

Introduction 1

Chapter 1: Cryptocurrency Basics 3

Chapter 2: Money Versus Cryptocurrency 13

Chapter 3: Uses of Cryptocurrency 17

Chapter 4: How to Buy and Sell Cryptocurrency 23

Chapter 5: Beginners Advice 31

Chapter 6: Top Cryptocurrencies In 2017 41

Chapter 7: Cryptocurrency Myths 47

Chapter 8: Trading and Investing in Cryptocurrency 53

Chapter 9: Where and How to Store Cryptocurrency 61

Crypto Conclusion 69

INTRODUCTION

I wrote this book to explain the basics that anyone would need to know about cryptocurrency. Cryptocurrencies have exploded in interest and value over the past few months, but since they are still new, many people are not familiar with what they are or how they work. This book will give you many of the basics that you need to really understand cryptocurrencies and to even begin using them yourself.

We are going to spend quite a bit of time looking over cryptocurrencies in this book and how you can benefit from using them. This book will start with some of the basics of cryptocurrency, such as how Blockchain technology runs the networks, the different types of cryptocurrencies, how to purchase your own coins to use on the network and how cryptocurrencies compare to fiat (or traditional currencies).

There are also some more advanced topics available including how to choose a wallet to store your cryptocurrency coins and how to invest in for profit and long or short term. Whether you are just getting started or you have been working with these coins for a bit and want to take them to the next level, this book is going to have the information that you need to get started.

CHAPTER 1

CRYPTOCURRENCY BASICS

Over the past few years, cryptocurrencies have really taken interest over the world. It wasn't long ago that these seemed like a silly idea, something that would never take off or something to not be trusted. But now, people all around the world are using cryptocurrencies and it's likely that they will continue to use them for many years to come.

If you are not familiar with using cryptocurrencies or have never used them before, the information may seem a bit overwhelming. Let's take some time to review the basics of cryptocurrency.

Blockchain Technology

The overall technology that helps to keep Bitcoin and other cryptocurrencies up and running is the blockchain. This is basically the ledger that is going to store all of the transactions inside the system so that users are able to look at it at any time. The ledger will be coded so that it is harder to see who did each transaction, but any user in the network will have access to it.

When you sign up for Bitcoin or one of the other currencies, you are going to start your own personal blockchain. You will be sent a block and it will fill up as you complete more transactions; whether you are making purchases, receiving payment, or ordering more Bitcoin. Once the block is filled up, it is going to become permanently stored in the network and you will receive a brand new piece of the block.

Each person is going to have their own blockchain and some will have a longer blockchain if they do a lot of transactions on the network, and some will have a smaller blockchain if they don't spend much time on the network. Once a block is done, it is going to be sent over to the networks blockchain and will join that ledger as well. The blockchain is great at holding onto all the information that you need for transactions and can get it done in a matter of minutes.

The blockchain is also able to keep all of this information safe and secure. With the help of miners, each transaction is changed to a special code (Bitcoin and other cryptocurrencies have rules in place to make sure that the code is legitimate and that it will keep the information safe). Once the miner is done, they are rewarded for their time so it becomes a win-win for everyone involved.

The blockchain is a really innovative technology that is already changing the world and is sure to do so more in the future. It is basically a ledger to hold onto information about all the transactions that occur on these online currency networks, but it is much more efficient compared to the ledgers used by financial institutions and banks in the real-world.

Terms to Know

Before you get too far into the world of cryptocurrencies, it is a good idea to learn about some of the terms so that you understand what we are talking about along the way. Some of the terms that can help you to get started on cryptocurrencies include:

- **Exchange**: these are the sites that you can use to purchase and sell cryptocurrencies. <u>The most popular one in North America is Coinbase.</u>

- **Fiat**: this is the traditional currency or the government issued currency of a country. It would include options like the Euro and the US Dollar

- **Blockchain**: this is the technology that runs Bitcoin and other cryptocurrencies. The blockchains are going to be distributed ledgers that are secured through code. They are available to everyone to look through, but the data owners are the only ones who can make updates to the data. The blockchain is going to hold all the information about all transactions on the network.

- **Node**: this is any computer that possesses a copy of the blockchain. If you sign up for Bitcoin or another currency, you would become a node because you hold a part of that currencies blockchain.

- **Mining**: this is the process of trying to solve the next block to keep information safe. It will require a lot of computer processing, but the payout is huge.

- **Fork**: this is when a blockchain is split up into two chains. This happens when there are new governance rules that are placed into the code.

- **Sharding**: this is a scaling solution for blockchain. Every node in the blockchain will hold onto a copy of the blockchain and sharding will help the nodes have only a partial copy so that the network will work faster.

- **Software wallet**: this is a storage container that will hold onto your cryptocurrency, but it is only available as a file on the computer. There are several options for the user to choose from.

- **Hardware wallets**: this is a device that will hold onto the cryptocurrency These are often seen as a safe way to hold onto the currency

- **Cold storage**: this is a way of moving your currency offline so that it is safer from hacking. There are a few ways to do this such as a hardware wallet, moving the files over to a USB drive, or printing out a QR code of your wallet.

- **Smart contract**: this is code that is used on a cryptocurrency network that can help bring together terms for two parties. There is no middleman because the smart contract will only execute when certain conditions are met.

The Benefits of Being Anonymous

One of the benefits that a lot of people enjoy when they are working with cryptocurrencies instead of traditional currencies is that they get to be anonymous. They can make purchases or receive money from others without everyone knowing what kind of transactions are going on and who is involved. The parties can go through and look at the blockchain to make sure the transactions were completed, but others will have a harder time figuring out this information.

In our modern world, many people have started moving to online shopping, online money transfers, and basically getting as much done online as they physically can. But while people are steadily moving online, the banks and financial institutions that we are dealing with are still in the past. They still post a lot of information in their databases about transactions, including personal information and credit card information. While these are supposed to be secure, they often fall short and it is not too hard for hackers to get onto the system.

On the other hand, cryptocurrencies have the benefit of using blockchain technology to help them keep personal information safe and secure. While there are some ways that hackers and others can find out who you are, especially if you make a lot of purchases, it is much safer than traditional banking methods. You can also choose to follow a few steps to make it harder for others to figure out who you are on the network.

Many people like the fact that they can remain anonymous when they are shopping online. While some people do take advantage of this for personal gains, such as performing criminal activities, most people use this to help keep their identities and payment information safe.

Reasons To Use Cryptocurrencies

There are a lot of reasons that people will choose to work with cryptocurrencies rather than some of the fiat currencies that they may be used to. First, they like that they can remain anonymous and not have everyone knowing what they do with their money. This is something that is hard for people to do with most fiat money and so they will move online and use one of the available cryptocurrencies.

The fact that these currencies don't rely on a central governing authority, whether that is a government agency or a bank or another financial institution, has a lot of appeal to many people as well. They are tired of having someone in the middle of their business, adding more fees and slowing down the process of commerce. With the help of blockchain technology, you get to enjoy all the safety and security that you need when working with purchases, without any interference or any middleman.

Cryptocurrencies are often really good for investing. Since this is a brand new form of currency, a lot of people are finding that there are many ways that they can benefit when they choose to invest in currency. They can do forex trading and hold onto the currency until it is worth more money, they can invest in blockchain technology, or even invest directly in the currency that they are interested in. There are so many different options when it comes to investing in cryptocurrency, there is a method for almost anyone out there, long term or short term. The only element many new users have to get over is the fact that this is all intangible currency and NEW.

Working with cryptocurrencies can also be way more efficient than working with banks and other intermediaries. There isn't the issue with having to work with a middle man, so you get the benefit of saving time and money. The transactions are done almost immediately, and you are able to verify all the information with the help of blockchain. While banks and other financial institutions may make you wait a few days before the transaction is complete, you will be able to work with these cryptocurrencies and get the transactions done in just a few minutes.

As you can see, there are many things to enjoy when you choose to work with a cryptocurrency, rather than relying on a fiat currency. All of these benefits and more are why people are choosing to switch over to some options like Bitcoin and Ethereum.

The Risks of Cryptocurrencies

There are a lot of great benefits to using cryptocurrencies over traditional currencies. You can remain anonymous and make it hard for other people to know what you are up to online. You can use a currency that doesn't have a government agency or a bank controlling how it works. You can even trade with people all over the world without all the transaction fees like you may have been used to.

With that being said, there are some risks that come with using cryptocurrency. It is relatively safe, but there are a few things that you have to be careful about including:

- **Government interventions**: governments across the world have taken different approaches to how they handle cryptocurrency. Some are embracing this form of currency and are even adopting some of their own version to help their own economies grow. Others, like the United States, are going after people who use Bitcoin and other currencies because they want to catch people who are avoiding taxes with this option. Understand how your government is responding to cryptocurrency in your country and learn what your responsibilities are all about.

- **Criminal activity**: there are some people who use the fact that they can remain anonymous on these sites to conduct criminal activities. This can include money laundering, selling illegal items, and avoiding taxes in their own country. Make sure that you are avoiding some of these criminal activities to reduce your risks on the network.

- **E-wallets**: for the most part these are safe and are a great way to hold onto you currency that you earn by using it. But there are some that are a bit more dangerous than others. Some people will create these e-wallets or even the mixing service sites, promising to hold onto the money and take care of it for you. While most of the companies are safe, some will just run off with your money and it is nearly impossible to get it back. Make sure to do your research and pick out reputable companies when working on these networks.

- **Watching out for the sellers**: the Bitcoin network, along with other cryptocurrency networks, are pretty new so understanding which sellers are legitimate and which ones aren't can be hard. While there are some safeguards in place to protect the buyer and the seller, you do need to be careful about those sellers who are more interested in taking your money and then running away.

As you can see, there are a few risks to working in cryptocurrencies, especially if you are just getting started and you don't do the right research ahead of time. For those who research cryptocurrencies ahead of time and learn how to work on the networks, they will find that their risks are reduced by quite a bit.

The Digital Currency in The Digital Age

Many people are interested in working with a digital currency. They like the idea of being able to make purchase and money online without having to go through a government agency or a bank. They like that this currency form is safe and effective and that they don't need to worry about hackers and other people getting ahold of their information, at least as much as they did with other forms of payment online. They like that they can send payments and money to anywhere in the world without having to pay all those extra fees.

There are so many benefits to working with cryptocurrency. It is designed for the modern world. While many people are still used to working in the past, going through banks and other intermediaries, this can cost a lot and can really slow down the process. But cryptocurrencies work to make this easier, helping transactions to get done quickly and providing a level of security than other traditional forms of payments.

As our world is entering into this new digital realm, with more things happening online all the time, it makes sense that a digital currency is rising to be the new medium to use in the digital world as well. Bitcoin and other cryptocurrencies will provide this benefit that many shoppers and others are looking for in a way that traditional banks and currencies just aren't able to do right now.

In 1995 very few people thought that the Internet would be where it is now. It has grown so quickly and vast that we have virtually run out of IP version 4 addresses and had to create a new IP addressing network (IPv6).

It is estimated the same growth and development is happening now in ecommerce and digital currency, think about it, we are already on the trajectory path. Where will all of this be in 5-10 years, YOU can position yourself now to benefit from this massive revolution!

CHAPTER 2

MONEY VERSUS CRYPTOCURRENCY

While most of us are used to working with fiat, or government issued, money, many people are starting to make changes to the money that they use. They are tired of letting a big bank or government control their money and they prefer the freedom that comes with cryptocurrency. This chapter is going to take a look at some of the differences that occur with cryptocurrency and fiat money and why the switch may be so tempting for some.

Central Banks and Fiat Money

Anyone who has been able to work in cryptocurrency for some time is familiar with some of the main differences between these online currencies and the traditional currencies. In most countries, there is some kind of paper currency, which is going to be run by the government or a central bank. These currencies are backed by silver and gold to help keep them stable.

There are some issues that come with this kind of currency though. First, many government agencies who control the fiat money will be able to manipulate it the way that they want. They can control inflation, watch what you spend your money on, and more. Many people don't like how these agencies can take over their money so easily and this helps them to decide to go with cryptocurrency instead.

Another issue is that central banks and the government controlling money is very expensive and inefficient. Big banks throughout the world lose millions of dollars each year because their accounting practices are not where they should be. And if a transaction gets finished within a day or two, it is considered fast, while a transaction on the blockchain could take just a matter of minutes. While fiat money is often seen as inefficient, many are moving over to cryptocurrencies because they are faster, cost less and are much easier to work with.

Advantages of Cryptocurrency

- **Secure**: The blockchain technology that most cryptocurrencies work on is considered safe and secure. It is designed to keep your information safe and with the help of the miners who control the system, you know that it is hard for hackers and others to steal your information or even trace it back to you.

- **Anonymous**: one reason that a lot of people are switching from fiat money over to cryptocurrency is that it helps them to stay anonymous. There are a few steps that you need to take to increase this anonymity, but overall, it is much easier to stay hidden on a cryptocurrency network than it is with a bank.

- **Quick**: cryptocurrency transactions are often quick. We have all sent a payment to someone through a traditional bank or financial institution and know that it can take a few days to even process. This really slows down the flow of commerce and can be really frustrating. Cryptocurrencies use blockchain technology to speed up this process. Transactions on cryptocurrency networks can often take just a few minutes rather than a few days, making it quick and efficient.

- **Decentralized**: when working with cryptocurrencies, you don't have to worry about a central authority, like a bank or a government agency, controlling the currency. Fiat currency is usually controlled by one of these entities, but this makes transactions inefficient. The benefit of working with cryptocurrency is that you don't have that central authority controlling all the money. Instead, a mathematical equation and a code will control all the money that is found in the cryptocurrency of your choice.

- **Easy to use**: unlike the traditional banking sources in our modern world, working with cryptocurrency is pretty easy. You just need to join the network that you want to use and set up a wallet to hold onto your coins. Once that is done, you are ready to start sending or receiving coins on the network. You don't have to jump through hoops to get it done, you don't have to show a lot of information, and it doesn't take several days for the money to transfer.

Decentralized Nature of Cryptocurrency

One of the benefits of working with cryptocurrency is the fact that it is decentralized. Banks, financial institutions or governments are able to decide how much the money's worth and when to print more, everything that has to do with fiat money.

Cryptocurrencies are different; these currencies have removed the controlling agent that is found in fiat money and changed it over to a mathematical equation. There is a code written about how the coins can be used, how many coins are available for people to use (and there can't be more created), and even how these coins can be released (through the miners).

People like cryptocurrencies because they don't have to worry about someone getting into their business or slowing down the whole process. Most of us are used to dealing with the government or waiting forever for a bank transaction to go through. These are not issues that you will deal with when working on cryptocurrency, which is a big draw to why so many people choose to go on these networks rather than continue working with fiat money.

CHAPTER 3

USES OF CRYPTOCURRENCY

Cryptocurrency is not just found in a small niche online that only a few people are able to use. In fact, the technology that helps run these online currencies is so innovative, that it is starting to take over many other areas of our financial world. This chapter is going to take some time to look at the various uses of cryptocurrency and how it is changing the way we do business in everyday life.

E-commerce, Business and Local Merchants

There are so many ways that cryptocurrencies can be used and the reasons just keep growing. In fact, people have begun to invest in blockchain technology because this is the part of cryptocurrencies that will have the biggest impact on our financial futures and the way that we conduct business in the future. But even today, there are some big uses for cryptocurrency and it is already shaping the way that businesses behave.

E-commerce

E-commerce is probably going to see the biggest change when it comes to cryptocurrency. Currently, when we want to shop online, we have to visit the store that we want to shop with, pick out the products we want to use, and then provide them with a lot of personal information, including our names, addresses, and our credit card information just to get the product.

This information is then stored inside the merchant's system, and as we have seen over the years with a wide variety of data breaches, this information is not necessarily the safest when it is stored in this way. Hackers are more than happy to get onto whatever system the store is using and take all your personal information to use for themselves. This is not really an efficient way to shop and has limited the trust that people have for many companies.

Things are a little different with cryptocurrency. It is possible to shop online and keep your information safe. Blockchain networks are designed to help keep all the information safe and with the help of the miners, these transactions are coded and stored in an extremely secure manner. No longer do you need to worry about your personal information just sitting there for someone to take thanks to this great technology.

In the future, it is likely that more e-commerce sites are going to start implementing blockchain technology. This will allow them to build up more trust with their customers and can make it safer to use their websites without as much risk of hackers getting on. There are not many companies who have this technology right now, but it is likely to continue growing in the future. Just another way that the world of cryptocurrency is going to change so many aspects of the way we do business in the future.

Business

The world of finance and business are going to change quickly once they start to modify and use the blockchain technology. Many of them are still in the past, using a ledger and accounting systems that just don't work that well for them or for the customer. These ledgers have a few problems. The first one is that they are slow; it takes a few days for the transactions to go through and this really slows down the buying and selling process. This can be frustrating to a lot of people who may do online purchases. We are used to the world where things should be instant, but instead, they are still considered slow.

Another issue is that these ledgers are not that secure. Our information is present on these ledgers and all someone needs to do is access the system to see it. They will see your credit card information, your name, and even address and more for each transaction. The blockchain technology that is currently applied to cryptocurrencies is able to hide your information, while still making it transparent so that the transactions you use won't automatically be linked back to you.

Big banks often lose millions of dollars each year because of accounting errors and inefficiencies. The blockchain technology, if it is used properly, could solve some of these issues and make it easier for banks to lower their fees associated with errors and administration.

The good news is that there are already many developers who are working on blockchain platforms that can work for a variety of financial institutions. There are even some financial institutions who have already adopted these platforms in order to save themselves money and to provide better customer service overall. While the current technology may be too expensive or not the right fit for a lot of companies right now, it is sure to develop in the future.

Local Merchants

There are many local merchants who choose to work with these cryptocurrencies. Some are small enough that they will offer their products and services exclusively on the network of their choice (often Bitcoin right now since that is the most popular), for customers to use. Others will add this in as a new payment method. For example, they may accept cash, PayPal, and credit card and then they add on Bitcoin or another cryptocurrency for their customers.

Some of the bigger chain stores are choosing to join the cryptocurrency market as well, making it easier to use your coins at more places. Some stores still aren't accepting these kinds of coins, but you can use your coins to purchase gift cards to those stores, so there is an indirect way to use these coins and shop where you would like.

Trading and Investing

Many people are choosing to use cryptocurrency as a way to make money, rather than just as a way to make purchases without the hassles of big banks and government agencies. Investing is a great option with these currencies, especially since they are so new, and many people who take their time and do research find that it is a great way to make money while these currencies grow.

There are quite a few investment options that are available, and we will talk about these in more detail later on. Some people choose to buy stock in the cryptocurrency company and then earn dividends on that each year. You can find a company to invest in that is on the network (which works really well with Ethereum), or they can do forex trading and purchase coins today and then exchange it out when it is worth more in the future.

Since cryptocurrencies are so new, it is likely that even more investment opportunities are going to arise in the future. People are always looking for a way to make money and as these cryptocurrencies expand to other parts of the world and more people learn about them, it is likely that there will be quite a bit of money allocated and invested in cryptocurrencies.

CHAPTER 4

HOW TO BUY AND SELL CRYPTOCURRENCY

Before you are able to get started on one of the cryptocurrency networks, you need to find a way to acquire the coins. You can't just join a network and expect them to hand you a bunch of coins to use how you want, just like you can't go to a new country and expect to be handed a lot of money either. Luckily, it is pretty easy for users to get ahold of some coins, in whatever cryptocurrency they want to use so that they can get to work making purchases and transferring money on the network.

Working with Coinbase (https://CoinBase.com)

If you are interested in doing trades with digital currencies, you need to find some kind of platform that will allow you to trade with them and an intermediary that is able to communicate with whatever cryptocurrency network you want to work with. Most people will not have the technical knowledge in order to figure out how to communicate with the blockchain or even how to store the digital currency. This is where companies like **Coinbase** are going to come into place.

Coinbase is basically an exchange company for digital assets. It is there to provide users a venue to buy and sell digital currencies and they can also use this platform in order to send information about their transactions over to the blockchain network, which helps to verify these transactions. Right now, Coinbase is the platform to use for Litecoin, Ethereum, and Bitcoin and it can serve as a wallet for these three cryptocurrencies if you would like as well.

Coinbase is considered one of the largest exchanges for these cryptocurrencies out there and it is the only one available in the United States. It is able to operate exchanges for Litecoin, Bitcoin, and Ethereum in 32 countries and Bitcoin has expanded to even more countries that the other two have not reached yet. According to the Coinbase website, this platform is currently serving more than 8.2 million customers and has facilitated more than $6 billion worth of digital currency.

Working with Coinbase can be pretty simple. Most customers will not want to deal with all the technical aspects of exchanging their fiat currency for a cryptocurrency, and Coinbase will do the work for you. It even includes a wallet so you are able to store your Bitcoin without having to go to another place.

There are some disadvantages to using this type of exchange though. For example, when you use Coinbase, **you will not be anonymous on the service**. Your name is going to be attached to the account as will your bank account so it is easier for others to track you down. For those who aren't doing anything illegal, this really shouldn't be that big of a deal. And if you are not working directly with the blockchain, you will find that you will be limited on what you can do to ensure that verification of your transaction history. You are basically putting your trust with Coinbase as an intermediary. But for those who are new to the whole idea of cryptocurrency and who aren't comfortable doing the work on their own, Coinbase can be a nice way to just get in the game securely.

Before you are able to purchase or sell your cryptocurrency, you need to make sure that you have a credit or debit card attached to the count or you need to link up your bank account. If you would like to have a higher limit on the transactions that you are doing, it is best to use your bank account, but it does take a little bit longer to verify these transactions since it goes through a bank. **Keep this in mind because it will take a few days if you are using your bank account to see the information come up on your account.**

And when you are selling your coins, you need to remember that if you have a bank account, it could take another two to four days before you will see those proceeds show up on the bank account. Some people like to use their bank accounts because it allows them to have some higher limits, but it is important to realize some of the downsides.

On the other hand, you can also work with your debit or credit card. The limits are going to be a bit lower with this option, but it is easier to purchase the digital currencies because you can simply take the funds from the card and place them on your account. With these transactions, the coins are going to be in your wallet almost right away. You can also sell the Bitcoin over to a PayPal account if you have one, which is basically cashing out since the coin will be changed out for local currency. This is also going to be an instant transaction as well.

How To Sign Up For Coinbase

Signing up for Coinbase is pretty easy and it is not going to take you too long to get started. You just need to visit the website www.coinbase.com/signup to get started. From there, you need to give a little bit of information. It will ask for your first name and your last name as well as your email address. You will also need to provide your preferred password. Take some time with this and make sure that you pick out a password that is strong and secure and that you haven't used with any other website in the past so that no one else is able to get onto the account.

Before you can continue on, you need to go through and let Coinbase know what state you are from, agree that you are not a robot, and then certify that you are at least eighteen years old. Coinbase will send you a verification email to make sure this is your information before you can work on the next step. Make sure to check your email and click on the link to get you into the account.

From here, you will be welcomed to Coinbase and you can follow the guide for buying your first digital currency. You will need to choose whether you would like to complete your profile as an individual or as a business. As a business, you will need to submit an application so that Coinbase can look at your institution before getting you started.

We are going to complete this as an individual. You can click on that link. From here you can decide if you want to skip a few steps for now, or you can work through it, providing your phone number in this step. Once you place your phone number in, you will be given a verification number in the text that you are able to place in to prove your verification.

At this point, you are going to be able to see the Dashboard for Bitcoin. It should list how much the Bitcoin is worth and how much it has changed in the last month. You can also check out the value of Ethereum and Litecoin as well. You also have places for buying and selling the Bitcoin that you want to use, setting up your accounts, sending the money, tools, and other settings that you can use. This dashboard should give you all the information that you need to get started on the Bitcoin and Ethereum exchange.

Coinbase is one of the best sites that you can choose to exchange your fiat currency over to a cryptocurrency. It even has the capabilities to be an online wallet which can be nice for those who are just getting started out and aren't sure how to do some of the technical stuff on their own. Make sure to follow some of the steps in this section to help you get your own account set up right away.

How To Purchase Bitcoin

The first step for you to get Bitcoin is to sign up for your Coinbase account. Coinbase is one of the most secure places to store the Bitcoin as well so you don't have to worry about losing the coins or having to transfer them over to another wallet. It is also a great place to go for easy payments so that you can convert into and out of Bitcoin from whatever your local currency. Follow the steps above to help you set up a Coinbase account.

Once your Coinbase account is set up, it is time to connect your bank account. There will be a few steps for verification before you can continue. This is so that Coinbase is able to get your funds out of the account since the bank is going to ask for this information. Once all of the steps for verification are done, you will be able to start your purchase.

After you have gotten started with the first purchase, it is possible to complete your buy and get the Bitcoin delivered to you. The Sells are going to work in the same manner, but you will just reverse the steps. The price of the Bitcoin, as well as the other cryptocurrencies that you want to use, will change over time, so you will need to learn what the current exchange rate is before you get started.

After you see the exchange rate, you will be able to choose how much Bitcoin or other currency that you would like to purchase and place your order. Coinbase will take your information and then place the order. After everything has been verified, the Bitcoin will be changed over to your wallet and you should be able to use the coins as soon as you would like.

If you have earned coins, from your business, or you have just left these in your wallet and waited for the price to go up, you can go through the opposite process. You can place an order with Coinbase to convert the Bitcoin or another coin back into your traditional currency and the money will be put back into your bank account. Coinbase makes it easy to switch back and forth between the cryptocurrency and the traditional currency whenever you would like.

Receiving Coins

Most people who decide to work on one of these cryptocurrency networks will decide to go through a site like Coinbase in order to get the coins that they need to start. But there are some methods that you can use to receive the right coins without having to use any of your own money. For the most part, this is going to work the best for those who own their businesses and who start accepting cryptocurrency as a payment source.

If you already have a business up and running, it is pretty easy to start receiving the coins that you want to use. Just like you already accept credit cards and PayPal, you can decide to start accepting Bitcoin or one of the other cryptocurrencies as well. As your customers start to use these coins as their form of payment, your wallet will fill up and you can switch it over to the fiat currency of your choice, with the help of one of the exchanges, whenever you would like.

Another method that you can use is to find someone who will transfer some money over to your account. This could be something that you do with your work or between friends and family. There are some people who will use these networks, for example, to help send money to someone overseas without needing to pay all the exorbitant fees that banks often charge. They can send some Bitcoin or other cryptocurrencies over to the wallet of the other person, and then that second party can use them on the network or exchange them for their local currencies.

CHAPTER 5

BEGINNERS ADVICE

As a beginner, you are sure to have a lot of questions when it comes to using these cryptocurrencies. These currencies are pretty new and many people are not sure how they work or all of the parts that come with these currencies. The good news is that once you get into the network of your choice, you will find that it is actually pretty easy to work with them, whether you want to be a seller and receive the coins or you are using this as a place to shop. This chapter is going to take some time to look at a few of the basic parts that beginners can follow when they first get into the cryptocurrency network.

Web Wallets

Web wallets are often managed by third parties who will hold onto the public and private keys for all your coins. These often help you to keep track of the coins that you are using and will ensure that your transactions stay safe. There are a few different types of web wallets that you can choose from, such as the one available from Coinbase, but you should do some research to figure out which one will provide you with the right security and features that you are looking for.

While these web wallets are going to help you to manage your cryptocurrency, the trade-off is that you need to be able to trust that third-party with your personal information. They are responsible for keeping your private cryptocurrency keys safe and for maintaining the integrity of your wallet. You have to pick a good one or they are able to just run off with your money and there aren't any regulations or rules that keep you safe.

There are a lot of advantages to using these web wallets. You will find that they are easier to use compared to holding it all yourself. It also gives you the ability to bundle together transactions before they are pushed out into the blockchain, which can lower a number of fees that you pay for these transactions. These wallets will perform some internal transfers for zero fees, which is an attraction that many will offer to get more customers in.

Before you pick out a web wallet to work with, make sure to do some research. You want to make sure that they are going to take good care of your coins and that they are secure. If a web wallet wants you to give a lot of information, you should be careful because the more they have about you, the harder it is to keep your information safe.

Web wallets are a great option to work with, but you may want to consider working with some other options as well, such as hardware wallets and cold storage. This will be helpful because even secure web wallets can be attacked by a hacker and it is a good idea to have a backup option to keep your coins safe online.

Protecting Your Privacy

One of the reasons that so many people like to use cryptocurrencies is because it allows them to remain anonymous and keep their personal identity safe and secure. Unlike other online transactions, the blockchain is set up to help you protect your personal privacy. It is important to realize that there are a few steps that you need to take to protect that privacy.

Many beginners believe that these cryptocurrencies are completely secure and that they never have to take another step outside of signing up for the network. But, it is still possible for others, if they want to put in the effort, to figure out who is doing each transaction and can get ahold of your information in that manner. There are a few things that you can do to help with this.

First, make sure that your address doesn't relate back to your personal information. Signing up for an address that has your first and last name and other identifying information will make it easier for a hacker or someone else to link you back to your transactions.

Also, if you plan to do quite a few transactions, you may want to consider having a few different cryptocurrency addresses. According to the white paper that was released with Bitcoin, it is recommended that you set up a new address for each transaction that you do on the network. This is not always necessary, especially if you are only doing a few transactions on occasion, but for those who plan to be busy on these networks, it can help to keep you safer because it becomes a lot harder for someone to track you.

Cold Storage

Cold storage is something that you should definitely consider when it comes to using cryptocurrency. This storage is important because it adds a level of security to your coins, making it harder for hackers to get ahold of your information and use it how they wish. Since these cryptocurrencies are still pretty new, there isn't a lot of regulation in place for protecting users against theft or fraud. These are not all that common yet on these networks, but as Bitcoin and the other online currencies grow, it is likely to become a bigger problem.

And this raises the question, where should you store your coins to keep them safe? Technically, you are not able to store these coins since they are all digital and there aren't any paper versions available. Rather, they are going to be accessed through keys, which are codes and addresses, that are kept in your wallet. Thus, you need to keep your digital wallet, the part that is holding the private and public keys, safe from others.

There are a few methods that are available for securing your wallet, including cold storage, multi sign, backup, and encryption. Of course, the first thing that you should do to keep this wallet safe is come up with a strong password and you should take the time to back-up the wallet in case something happens.

Cold storage is definitely a method you should use to help protect your wallet and the coins inside of it. This type of storage basically means that you should store your coins offline, away from any access online. When you take your coins offline, you are able to really reduce the threat you face from hackers. It is a bit less convenient when it is time to backup or encrypts, but it is really one of the safest methods for keeping your coins safe. If you do want to backup and encrypt, you can choose cold storage for the coins that you want to save for later, and then keep a few online to make it easier for regular transactions.

There are a few methods that you can choose for cold storage. Some are easier to use than others, but all of them can be effective and the one you choose is completely up to you. Some of the options that you can pick for cold storage include:

- **Paper wallet**: this is a safeguard against a malfunction on your computer and against hackers. What it does is have you print off your private and public keys and the keep them on paper. In addition, these paper wallets are often going to have a QR code on them that you can scan if you want to quickly make a transaction. Since this paper is going to have all the information that is needed to spend your coins, it is going to be pretty safe and you won't have to worry about what goes on online.

- **Storage devices**: some people decide to put the information for their keys on a storage device such as a USB drive. These are fairly easy to work with, but you do need to take some extra precautions to make sure someone doesn't get ahold of them. Keep them away from the computer and perhaps leave in a deposit box or a safe.

- **Sound wallets**: sound wallets can help to keep your virtual currency safe. This technology is going to help keep your private keys secure by placing them in encrypted sound files on vinyl disks and CDs. You are able to get these codes of the audio files with the help of a spectroscope app.

- **Hardware wallets**: these are the preferred choice or cold storage. They are small devices, which are designed to be virus and water proof, and you can place the keys on there. BitSafe and Pi-Wallet are two examples of a hardware wallet.

The idea of a deep cold storage service is becoming popular as well. It was introduced as a service that is insured by an underwriter so it is going to provide protection against loss or theft. There is a drawback about this service because it requires address and identity proof of the person who is seeking this service. If you wish to remain anonymous, this service is not the best, but if you don't mind this as much and you are more worried about keeping the Bitcoin safe, then this is the right option for you.

Backing Up

In addition to working with cold storage and trying to protect your privacy while you are on these networks, you need to make sure that you are backing up your information on a regular basis, no matter what kind of cryptocurrency you are dealing with. Unlike a dollar bill or another fiat currency, the currency that we are dealing with online is basically just lines of code on your computer. If you have coins, like Bitcoins, saved on your computer and it ends up dying, <u>your money is gone without a trace</u>. And with each coin being worth so much right now, it is no wonder that backing up your information is important.

You have to take the right precautions to ensure that your money is safe. Otherwise, if something happens to your computer and it ends up dying, you are going to lose all the information that makes up your currency, which could mean a lot of money. The best option is to use a backup imaging software. ShadowProtect is a good option because it is going to take a full image of the whole system and then will save that information. It can even keep the information that your cryptocurrency coins are made up and encrypt that information to keep it safe.

ShadowProtect is good because, in addition to helping backup the information that you have on your computer, it will take these backups at incremental times. This means that if you are messing around and accidentally delete the coins in your wallet, you should have them saved in one of your earlier backups so it is easier to recover them.

The trick to backups is that you need to do them on a regular basis, otherwise they do become worthless. If you are making a lot of transactions with Bitcoin, it doesn't make much sense to just do one backup and then avoid doing this for the next year, or the information will be outdated. When it comes to your coins or any money for that matter, you should make sure that you are doing many backups on a regular basis.

Another option is to have a few formats of your backups ready. The ShadowProtect option, and other software like it, are digital formats, but it is also a good idea to have a paper trail as well. This ups your level of protection so that you can keep some physical copies of the computer and then also have the digital copies to be safe. The more proofs that you have about your coins, the easier it can be if something does go wrong and you lose the information.

Preventing Hackers

When you are working with cryptocurrencies, you do need to be careful with hackers. This method of currency is considered much safer than some of the other options out there, but it is still a place where hackers will go to try and get your personal information. There are so many people who are on these networks and if you are not careful with your information and the transactions that you use, you could have a hacker get ahold of your information.

There are a few things that you can do to prevent hackers getting ahold of your information. The first step is to make sure that your credentials for getting onto your cryptocurrency network are secure. Don't pick a common address that will state exactly who you are and don't use passwords that are simple or are already on a few of your accounts. If you do this, it is easier for the hacker to get onto your cryptocurrency account if they happen to hack one of your other accounts.

Using cold storage and backing up your information can work out well too. There are a lot of beginners who will keep their coins online because this is easier. But the longer that these coins are kept online, the more appealing they are to hackers to get ahold of. If you store them on your hardware or through a storage option like cold storage, they are much harder for the hacker to get ahold of.

Hackers are always trying to get your personal information and if you don't keep that information safe, you will find that they can get your coins and use them how they want. Cryptocurrency is becoming a big market and it is really appealing to hackers to try and get this information. Leaving it all online, without the proper security, is just asking for a hacker to come onto the site and steal the information so make sure to take the precautions that you need to keep hackers away.

CHAPTER 6

TOP CRYPTOCURRENCIES IN 2017

Cryptocurrencies are becoming the new way to make purchases and receive payments online. They are often reliant on the blockchain technology, which helps to make them secure and can get payments done in just a few seconds without needing to have a bank or another intermediary in the middle taking fees and slowing down the whole process. Let's take a look at some of the top cryptocurrencies in 2017!

Bitcoin and Lite Coin

Bitcoin was one of the first cryptocurrencies to be developed in 2009. It was designed to be an online alternative to traditional currency, without the control of a central government or bank to determine how the currency will work. People like to use this system because it is fast, it isn't controlled by a government agency and the fact that the blockchain makes it more secure and safe compared to other methods of making purchases online.

Lite Coin is similar to the Bitcoin, but it has been developed to help out with some of the issues that have come up with the Bitcoin. For example, Lite Coin is designed to handle more transactions because it can generate blocks faster than ever before. This would require a big update to the Bitcoin network for it to be able to keep up with this. Many people like this though because it speeds up the transactions between the merchant and the seller.

Bitcoin Cash

Bitcoin Cash is part of the official split that has recently occurred with Bitcoin. It is actually a competing virtual coin, but most people don't understand what the difference between Bitcoin Cash and regular Bitcoin is. Bitcoin Cash first split off from Bitcoin because there was an ideological divide between the people who were using it. There was a vocal minority who saw some issues with Bitcoin and choose to solve these issues by splitting off and starting with their own cryptocurrency.

There have been some benefits with working on this because it has helped to renew some excitement in the market. It has even helped to raise the price of Bitcoin in the process. Bitcoin Cash is becoming popular and now investors are interested in how they could purchase Bitcoin Cash. There are some people who are able to get ahold of these coins without needing to place a purchase.

<u>Coin owners who already have their own private keys for regular Bitcoin are able to take those keys and use it to access the Bitcoin Cash.</u> If you don't already have one of these keys, you will need to look at the wallet that you are using and see if they are considered Bitcoin Cash Friendly. <u>If they are, you can get ahold of the Bitcoin Cash without too many issues.</u>

For those who are just entering the cryptocurrency market, it is possible to purchase some of these coins as well. Coinbase is a good exchange, but right now it is not accepting the Bitcoin Cash and Bitfinex is not accepting it quite yet either, although they state that they will monitor the situation and see how it progresses. Working with your wallet is one of the best ways to work with getting the coins that you need with Bitcoin Cash.

Altcoin

Altcoins are going to be pretty much any of the cryptocurrencies that are not part of the Bitcoin network. Bitcoin is often considered one of the best cryptocurrencies because it has been around for several years, but there are a lot of other cryptocurrencies that are available and they often help to fill some kind of need that customers need help with. Some of the most popular altcoins include:

Ethereum

Another Altcoin that you can choose to work with is Ethereum. This is another blockchain company that works similar to Bitcoin but has a different purpose. It works with the cryptocurrency token called an Ether, which you can transfer between accounts and to compensate the seller if a purchase is made.

This type of currency is used in a slightly different way than Bitcoin and some of the others. With this cryptocurrency, the users will often use the Ether in order to fund start-up companies, particularly those who are creating apps and other online software. The company can list information about what they are designing and what they are going to use the funds for and others can use their Ether to fund the startups that appeal best to them.

Ripple

Ripple is another cryptocurrency that you can work with. a Ripple is a type of open payment network where the currency is transferred. Even though it is still pretty new, the goal of this system is to enable the users to break out of the "walled gardens" that are our current financial networks, such as banks, credit cards, and other financial institutions that are restrictive with monthly fees and processing delays.

According to their website, the company that designed ripple wanted to use the currency in order to address our economies current issue with money flowing freely. Many people are frustrated with working with banks and other financial institutions that seem to impede the free flow of money through fees and long delays in processing. The goal of Ripple is to build a currency that is digital and decentralized so that users can avoid some of these issues.

This is similar to the Bitcoin platform in that both of them are digital currencies that were designed on mathematical formulas and both have a limited amount of coins that can be used on the system. You can even use them to move money from one account to another without a third party needs to be present and both will provide security to make sure that counterfeit coins are not getting into the mix.

There are some differences between the two types of coins though. Ripple is more of a complement, rather than a competitor, to Bitcoin. There is even an option to use Ripple for Bitcoin. The network of Ripple is going to be a bit different than what you may have found with Bitcoin because it is going to make it much easier to transfer any currency form, whether this is a cryptocurrency or a traditional one like the dollar or a Euro.

NEM

The next option that we will look at is called NEM. This is a coin that was developed in 2016 and was released with the goal of becoming a public and a private blockchain. Unlike the popular Bitcoin, it uses a proof of work algorithm that is going to reward miners for how much hashing power they place in a block so they are rewarded based on how much they provide to the community.

NEM is going to be based on three different things include the cluster nodes, the vested amount of NEM, and the net transfers. When we are talking about net transfers, we are talking about any transactions that were made in the past month. The vested NEM is going to be how much a person has been about to save of these coins. And then the cluster nodes are going to be the accounts that are largely active with others.

Each account on this network is going to have unvested and vested NEM. The importance that you have on this network is going to be based mostly on the vested amount in your account. When you receive a new NEM in a transaction, it will be considered unvested. A good way to think about this is like a checking account where you will receive NEM that is unvested and then a savings account for the NEM that are vested. Every day, about ten percent of the unvested NEM is going to move over to a vested status.

Then, when you send over NEM to others, such as a money transfer or a purchase, you are going to take a bit from some of your unvested and your vested balances. This is done to help discourage really fast trading. In addition, if someone receives NEM and then tries to keep it so that they get a higher score, they are going to end up losing some of the scores because hoarding is not encouraged.

CHAPTER 7

CRYPTOCURRENCY MYTHS

Since cryptocurrencies are pretty new and many people have not had a chance to use them yet, there are a lot of myths that have sprung up about these currencies. People often don't understand how they work, so they are worried that the cryptocurrency may not be safe, may be a scam, or that something else may be wrong with them. This chapter will go through some of the cryptocurrency myths to give you a better understanding of how these currencies work.

"It's Not Backed By Gold or Silver - So It's No Good."

One thing that makes some people nervous about using cryptocurrencies is that there is no physical material that backs it up. With traditional currencies, you have the backing of silver and gold, or the government's promise and backing. While it doesn't work this way in practice, in theory, you could take some of your money to the bank and get a certain amount of gold or silver back in the process. But Bitcoin and the other cryptocurrencies are not designed to work this way.

Instead, these cryptocurrencies are designed through code. The code will state how much they are worth and in many cases, there are only so many of each coin available to use. For example, Bitcoin was designed with just 21 million coins available, but many of them have not been mined yet and are still not in use. This helps to keep the currency stable without needing the backing of anything else.

Only criminals use it

Yes, there are some criminals who do work with cryptocurrencies. They like the fact that they can remain anonymous on the network and conduct their activities with a limited chance of someone being able to tell it is them. They will avoid taxes, money launder, and even sell items that are considered illegal, whether those items are illegal in their country or in the country they are sending the items to. The system is set up to help make things a bit easier for criminals to get away with these things.

But, for the most part, those who are on these networks are there because they want to use the cryptocurrency for legitimate purchases. They like all the features and the ability to make more purchases throughout the world than they were ever able to do before. And most people are doing it all legally, purchasing products that they are allowed to use in their countries and claiming the money they make in taxes. While some criminals may be on these networks, most of the people who are there are law-abiding citizens.

"A Government Agency Controls It"

We are used to working with money that has some kind of government control over it. This is the way that we have dealt with money in the past and we know that it is backed by gold and silver and the word of our government. This is not true with Bitcoin and all of the other cryptocurrencies, although there are a few governments who are trying to develop their own version to use in their countries.

The fact that a government agency is not controlling Bitcoin and Ethereum and all the options is one of the main benefits that people enjoy when they are working with cryptocurrency. They are tired of a bank or a government agency deciding the inflation rates or how much their money's worth at the end of the day. They like that freedom, the freedom of being able to earn and send money without having Big Brother there messing around with things.

"It Is a Scam"

Cryptocurrencies are brand new and this can sometimes make them a bit scary and misunderstood by those who are not familiar with them. They are located only online, with no paper counterparts for you to use. They aren't controlled by a government agency, just computer code. They allow you to remain anonymous, rather than having all your personal information stored where any hacker can get ahold of it. It can be used for purchases all around the world, without having to worry about it taking too long for the payment to go through or the high transaction fees.

All of this is stuff that we just aren't used to when it comes to our money and some people believe that it is too good to be true. But in fact, cryptocurrency is able to deliver on all its promises and more, making it the perfect choice to use. There are still going to be some that believe that it is a scam, but it is actually a safer way to make and receive payments than anything you have used in the past. And if you ever decide that you don't want to work with the cryptocurrency again, you can always exchange it back out for the fiat money that you want.

"Cryptocurrencies Can't Be Hacked"

This is a common misconception. <u>It is possible for all cryptocurrencies to be hacked.</u> These cryptocurrencies are designed with the help of a code so as long as the hacker is able to get on the network and use the code how they want, it is possible for them to hack the cryptocurrency. But there are some safeguards in place that help keep the network a bit safer than what you find with traditional currencies.

First, the mining process can help to keep information about your transactions safe. The codes that go on the blockchain are set up so that if someone messes with even one number or letter in the code, it is going to mess with everything else, making it impossible to go undetected. You can also choose to work with e-wallets that provide extra protection and security to make sure that your information is not being hacked.

Sometimes it is best if you choose to use cold storage to hold onto your currency, especially if you are not using it all that often. This allows you to keep the currency off the computer so a hacker is not able to take it and use it how they want when you aren't around.

"Transactions in Cryptocurrency Are Untraceable"

Many people think that it is impossible to trace cryptocurrencies, but this is not true. There are ways to remain pretty anonymous on the network and keep your information safe, but the cryptocurrencies themselves can be traced. Remember that Bitcoin and the other networks want to make sure that they are transparent because this helps to build trust between them and the users so making it impossible to trace the currency at all can make this goal hard.

All of the currencies that you use are going to be traceable. They all have histories on them, which is why some people want to switch them out to make sure transactions are not traced back to them. The ledger system with blockchain will also keep track of transactions that occur on the network, which also helps to trace the currency.

"Merchants Won't Accept Cryptocurrency"

There is a little bit of truth in this one, but it is not as bad as some people think. You may not be able to go into every traditional merchant in the country and make a purchase, but you may be surprised at how many already accept Bitcoin and other cryptocurrencies as a form of payment. Think of it like a specialty credit card, like MasterCard. Not every merchant you go to is going to accept it, but there are plenty of options that do

When these cryptocurrencies first began, there were only a handful of merchants who were willing to accept these currencies at all. It was a new idea and one that many were not that familiar with to start. But now that Bitcoin and some of the other cryptocurrencies are starting to grow, it seems like more merchants are jumping on board as well.

There are several ways that you can purchase items through many merchants with the help of Bitcoin. The first option is to look through the Bitcoin (or whatever cryptocurrency you want to use) and see what merchants are available on that network. There are some popular merchants that already work through these networks and you are able to make your purchases without a lot of hassle.

There are also a few merchants that you can use cryptocurrencies with but they aren't available online. They can use special machines that will scan your QR code in a store and take the Bitcoin out of your wallet. These are growing in popularity with some of those companies who want to reach out to the cryptocurrency crowd but who haven't found ways to be online or on the right network yet.

You will find that there are ways around the stores that don't accept cryptocurrency as a payment right now. For example, Amazon doesn't accept these kinds of currencies. But you can take your Bitcoin and other cryptocurrencies, purchase some gift cards and then use those to purchase items on Amazon. This may not be the most direct method, but it helps you to open up even more merchants to work with.

CHAPTER 8

TRADING AND INVESTING IN CRYPTOCURRENCY

While many people are happy with going on these online currencies and making purchases, receiving money, and so on while keeping their information private, there are some investors who are seeing this as a great way to make profits. They can choose to invest directly in the company, invest in the technology that runs these companies, and so much more. This chapter is going to take some time to look at the basics of how to invest in cryptocurrency.

Day Trading

When you are day trading in the cryptocurrency world, you are placing a bet on whether the price of the coin is going to go up or down throughout the day. Day trading is a process where you will buy into the market that you want at the beginning of the day and then sell at some point during that same day before the market closes. In most cases, day trading is going to occur in the country where the trader lives and they need to make all of their purchases and sells before the close of the day.

Now, the biggest issue with day trading is that instead of just being open during the day, this is an active market all day long, even at night, and it can be really influenced by what is going on in other countries. So your day trading may turn into night trading as well if you don't set up the right strategy.

There are some exchanges that have developed the ability to place limit orders and stop orders. What this means for the trader is that you can decide what you want to do, either buy or sell, once a currency hits a certain price ahead of time and when your order is ready. Limit orders can help you to plan a bit ahead, and even sleep, even if you think there may be some movements that occur in the market overnight.

For example, let's say that towards the end of the day, you purchase into the currency at $20. If you think that the price of that is going to rise overnight, you would place a limit order when the currency hits a price of $21. If you want to be protected in case it dips down, you could place a limit order so if the currency reaches $19, you will sell. With these orders, the trade is going to happen, even if you aren't there, which can protect your investment.

Since cryptocurrencies can be used all throughout the world, it is possible for a big movement in prices to occur all around the world. These markets never close, because someone is awake somewhere in the world, and there isn't just one market, which can make things like day trading difficult. It can be difficult to trade all of the time, you need to sleep at some point, and you really need to have a good idea of how these different markets work if you want to be successful.

Long Term Investing

There are a lot of options that you can choose when it comes to long term investing with cryptocurrency. This is a new type of investment opportunity, but that means that you are going to be able to earn a lot of money in a variety of ways, especially if you get in now before the market becomes saturated. Some of the best long-term investments that you can work with include:

Invest In The Cryptocurrency Company

The most direct way that you can invest is to purchase stocks in the cryptocurrency company of your choice. For example, if you want to work with Bitcoin, you would purchase a part of the Bitcoin company through stocks. Bitcoin and other cryptocurrencies are quickly rising so getting into the game early on, you can see your dividends grow quite a bit.

Invest In The Blockchain Technology

The blockchain technology is really the backbone for all cryptocurrencies. This is the ledger that keeps track of all the transactions that occur in the system and establishes the trust for how these networks work. <u>The good news is that the blockchain technology is applicable in many other industries outside of cryptocurrency, which means the potential for a big future upside is likely.</u>

You don't have to know how to work blockchain or even how to write blockchain code in order to profit. <u>You can find a company who is developing a new blockchain platform and choose to invest</u>

with them. You can work on the smart contract or a traditional way in order to earn either a part of the profit or some of the interest rate from these platforms.

Forex Trading With Cryptocurrency

Just like you are able to invest in currencies from across the world, you can use forex trading for the cryptocurrency. For this to work, you would take the fiat currency in your area and then purchase the cryptocurrency of your choice. You will need to hold onto this currency for some time (there are fluctuations that occur in the market). Once the cryptocurrency raises enough in price, you will exchange it back out to your fiat currency and keep the profit.

A good example of this is with Bitcoin. Back in February 2017, the price of one Bitcoin was $2,500. You could take the $2,500 and earn one Bitcoin (or use whatever amount of money you would like to invest). Those who held onto their Bitcoin for a bit would be able to earn money in the process. If those same people exchanged the Bitcoin back out for their fiat currency today, we are using USD here, they would earn $4,000 USD. This means that the value of their money has increased by $1,500 in just six months.

There is some up and down movement in the cryptocurrency world though, which is why you do need to stick with it for the long term. For example, on July 6, 2017, Bitcoin was worth $2,600, but by the 19th of that month, it was down to $1,900. Later in August, it had risen back up to $4,000 though. There is a steady increase in the price of these cryptocurrencies, but if you panic and get out of the market too quickly because of a little downtick in the market, you are going to end up losing a lot of money.

Investing In a Startup Company

This one works really well with the Ethereum platform, which is set up to do these types of exchanges, but there are some other platforms that will allow you to invest in a start up company as well. You are able to take a look at the companies that are using that cryptocurrency (they may be using more than one as well), and then invest in helping their company grow.

If you do go with this option, make sure that both parties are working with a smart contract. What this means is that you will sign a contract that will execute when certain conditions are met. This helps to protect both parties without needing to have a third party in the middle, costing a lot of money. Make sure that you and the other person have set out all the conditions of the investment so that they receive the money they need to get started and you will earn back on it as soon as the right time occurs.

Create Smart Contracts

As we mentioned above, there is a big demand for smart contracts in the cryptocurrency world. These help two parties to have a solid contract between them without having to worry about hiring a lawyer or another party that will cost them a lot of money. But before these contracts are able to work, you need to have someone who can create them.

For someone who is good at computer programming, creating a smart contract can be the perfect option. You just need to write out the template and the code that will get this contract to execute. Once that is done, the parties will be able to pay you a small fee for the use of the contract, put in their information, and they are all set.

Choose an Exchange

Before you decide to start investing in cryptocurrency, you need to pick the exchange that you are going to work with. Some of the companies that trade on Bitcoin and the other cryptocurrencies are going to be available on the Nasdaq and on the New York Stock Exchange, but many of them will not. The good news is that there are some exchanges that are growing that will allow you to work specifically with these cryptocurrencies.

Before you choose the exchange that you want to work with, there are a few things that you can look over to help you out with that decision. The first place to look at which exchanges are offering the trades that you want to work with. If you want to do a specific type of trade or work with a specific company, you need to look at this since not all the exchanges are going to offer every option, especially right now at the beginning.

The next thing you need to look at is some of the fees that you will have to pay for the different trades on each exchange. Most of them are going to be pretty similar, but there will be some differences. A quarter percentage difference between two companies may not seem like a huge deal, but when you start doing a lot of trades, this is going to quickly add up to a lot of money. The cheapest option is not always the best, but taking the time to research your choices and picking out the one that offers the deal can always help you to save money.

Take some time to talk to a few brokers ahead of time as well. There are a lot of brokers who are starting to move into the field of cryptocurrency because it is becoming such a big way for some people to make money. You should find a broker you like, someone who gives advice that you trust and that you are comfortable working with, and then see which exchange they are working on. Sometimes if you are not sure the best exchange, finding the right broker and then going with their exchange can be the best bet.

And always make sure to do some research on the different exchanges. While most of these exchanges haven't had a ton of time to establish themselves since cryptocurrencies are so new, you can still get some information on them. Make sure that you are comfortable with their fees, that they provide many different options, and that you are going to be given a fair chance at seeing success.

CHAPTER 9

WHERE AND HOW TO STORE CRYPTOCURRENCY

One of the questions that you may have when you are first getting started with Bitcoin and some of the other cryptocurrencies are where and how you are going to store them. You want to make sure that you are able to easily access these coins any time that you would like, but you also have to worry about hackers and others getting onto the network and stealing your information. This chapter is going to take a look at some of the methods you can use in order to store your cryptocurrency to keep it safe and easy to use.

Types of Wallets

There are a lot of different options that you can use when it comes to storing your cryptocurrency coins. When you purchase the coins or receive a payment, you need to have some place where the currency can go and hold it for you. The cryptocurrency wallets are often the best places for you to get started because they will hold onto the coins until you are ready to use them.

There are a few wallets that you are able to choose from based on what kind of security you would like, what seems to be the easiest for you to work with, and how often you use the coins. Some of the most common types of wallets that you can use to store your cryptocurrency coins include:

- **Software wallets**: if you use your coins quite a bit to make a lot of purchases and to do a lot of other transactions, using a software wallet can be the best for you. There are a lot of software wallets that will hold your coins online for you and help keep track of your transactions all at the same time. Coinbase is a good place to start, but do some research to find the best software wallet for your needs.

- **Cold storage wallets**: if you are someone who doesn't use their cryptocurrency coins all that often, cold storage wallets are often the best. These allow you to just print off the information and store it somewhere else, far from your computer and the internet. Any time that you are ready to use the coins, you just need to bring your key out and use that information.

- **Hardware wallets**: if you don't use your coins that often, or you are worried about a hacker getting ahold of your information, you may want to go with a hardware wallet. These will store the coins off the internet, usually on the hardware of your personal computer. This makes it easily accessible to you, but ensure that a hacker or someone else won't get the coins, even if they are online.

Cold Storage

One option that you may want to use when working in cryptocurrency is called cold storage. What this means is that you are going to take your cryptocurrency coins and then store them, or the key that unlocks them, in an environment that is offline. This is a good choice to use if you don't plan to use the currencies right away. Hackers are often looking online and if they see an account sitting there that hasn't been touched in a long time, they are more likely to go for that account. With cold storage, you are able to store your currency away from the internet when they are not in use.

There are actually a few different methods that you can use to help with cold storage. Some of these include:

Paper wallets

These are the cheapest form of the cold wallet that is available and they are free to use. With this storage method, you will generate your private keys to the cryptocurrency offline, which helps to protect your security. And once the coins are transferred to the paper wallet, you are safe. Each cryptocurrency is going to have its own paper wallet type so take a look to see which one is the best for you.

Hardware wallets

This is another option that you can go with, but it will cost a little bit more to accomplish. The hardware wallet is going to be an electronic device. It is going to sign all the transactions you do through private keys that you will store online and you will be able to use the backup options that they offer if you need to recover the funds. KeepKey, TREZOR and Ledger Nano S are the best hardware wallets that you can pick. These are really popular so ordering one right away, there could be a few months wait on it, can be for the best.

USB drive

You can also store your cryptocurrency on a USB drive. This is considered an easy method to store the coins, but it is not always the safest. You just need to export and then save your keys on the USB drive. But if anyone gains access to the USB drive, they are going to have access to all the information that is present on your key so be careful with this one.

Desktop wallets

These wallets are going to keep your information on the computer, but it will only be present on your computer. You can use this to export the files of your encrypted private keys to an offline environment. You do need to be careful that others are not getting on your computer and accessing the information though.

Types of Coinbase

If you live in America, you will most likely work through the site Coinbase in order to purchase Bitcoin to get started. This is one of the leading exchanges in America for these cryptocurrencies and is often the place that people will go when they are just getting started with cryptocurrency.

One of the nice things about working with Coinbase is that it is not just an exchange company, <u>but also a Bitcoin wallet</u>. This can be nice for beginners who aren't sure how to get started because they can purchase their Bitcoin and then not have to worry about transferring it over to somewhere else. Coinbase is actually pretty large, operating an exchange between fiat currencies and Bitcoin in twenty-six countries with over 190 being able to use Coinbase as a storage wallet for Bitcoin.

Another option that is similar to Coinbase is known as Circle. This is a wallet service that was designed to be as easy as possible to use. It provides the users with the ability to purchase and sell Bitcoins instantly, either with their US bank account or a credit card. Many customers like using this one because it also has a version of this wallet available for iOS and Android.

These are the two most popular options for trading cryptocurrencies in America. They offer the chance to take your regular fiat currency and exchange them for Bitcoin or one of the other currencies and you can also exchange them back to fiat currency when you want. They also offer a safe and secure place to store your cryptocurrencies online, making it easy for beginners to get started.

There are some other options for Coinbase like companies throughout the world. In Singapore for example, Coinhako is popular. Each country will work with its own exchange company to help them change out their own personal fiat currency for the cryptocurrency that they want to use.

Importance of Storage and Avoiding Hackers

Finding a good storage for your cryptocurrency is one of the most important things to do when you work online. There are a lot of hackers and others who are hoping to get online and steal your information. It would be easy for them, especially if you don't pick out a good wallet or another storage place, to just get online and take your coins without a trace. But if you pick out a good storage place, your coins and your personal information are much safer but nothing is 100%, unfortunately.

There are a lot of different storage and wallet solutions for you to choose from, but how do you make the right decision? The first thing that you should look at is the security of the storage. Do they provide adequate security so that your information stays safe? Do they keep records of which coins come in and out? Have they had any recent data breaches?

Another thing that you can look at is whether the company takes your privacy seriously. One of the reasons that people choose to go with cryptocurrencies is because it will help to keep their personal information secure while they are online. If the wallet is storing your information and not doing it in the proper way (meaning that hackers can easily access it), you need to find another wallet or storage place right away.

You can also look at some of the other services that the wallet provides. Some will provide a mixing service so that the history of your Bitcoins or other coins are always moving around, making it harder to trace things back to you. There are some other features that you can work with as well to make sure that you are getting the security and the safety that you need.

Creating Your Own Hardware Wallet

A hardware wallet is going to be a special Bitcoin wallet which will be able to store all of the private keys of the user in a hardware device. There are a number of advantages to using the hardware wallet over the software wallets that most people like to use including:

- The private keys are going to be stored in an area of the microcontroller that is protected. This means that the keys won't be transferable out of the device as easily.

- These are immune to the viruses that are known to steal from software wallets.

- These wallets can be used interactively and securely, compared to a paper wallet which is something that needs to be moved over to software at one point or another.

- The software for these wallets is going to be open-sourced, which means that the user is able to validate the operation.

These wallets are helpful because they are going to store your information on the hardware of the computer rather than on some software that is located online. This may take a bit more time, but it can ensure that the information is going to stay as safe as possible.

<u>One of the easiest ways for you to create a hardware wallet is to visit the bitcoin.org website</u>. They provide you with a few different options for Bitcoin wallets, including those for your Desktop, your mobile device, the web and even hardware wallets that you may enjoy. Some of the best hardware wallets that are recommended for Bitcoin include: TREZOR, Ledger Nano S, Ledger Nano, KeepKey and Digital Bitbox.

These are just a few of the options available and you can choose to go with other types of wallets as well. Make sure that you do your research ahead of time. See what reviews each hardware wallet is receiving and learn whether they are secure with your information. You don't want someone else to get ahold of your cryptocurrency coins or your information.

Cryptocurrency has changed the way that we do business, but since most of the transactions are going to happen in the digital world with no paper versions available, it can be harder to properly store cryptocurrency.

CRYPTO CONCLUSION

There are so many different types of cryptocurrencies out there, you should choose one that fits your goals and personality. This book discussed the various cryptocurrencies and how to get started, how they work and even how to keep your information safe.

Unfortunately there is a lot more to learn about digital money. Any active investor or user MSUT stay informed when it comes to cryptocurrency and we tried to cover the bare basics in this book, but the importance of staying updated on latest technology and trends in cryptocurrency is paramount. This is a fast-emerging technology that has the potential to change traditional paradigms we have accepted as normal for a long time. While cryptocurrencies may be pretty new and many people may not understand how they work completely, they are currently making a big difference in the way our world works and it will only grow.

Finally, if you found this book useful in any way, a positive review on Amazon is always appreciated!

© DigitalMoney Technology

Stay Updated With Our Latest Cryptocurrency Books and Articles On Our Website.

Sign-Up For Our Email Updates and Receive a **FREE Discount Code For Any Paperback Book** Version Released and Fast Alerts to New FREE Book Promotions In The Future

https://DigitalMoney.Technology

www.ingramcontent.com/pod-product-compliance
Lightning Source LLC
Chambersburg PA
CBHW050013230526
45470CB00003B/942